8|11

Imagining the **Future**

GETTING AROUND
in the PAST, PRESENT, and FUTURE

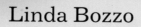

Linda Bozzo

Bailey Books
an imprint of
Enslow Publishers, Inc.
40 Industrial Road
Box 398
Berkeley Heights, NJ 07922
USA
http://www.enslow.com

Bailey Books, an imprint of Enslow Publishers, Inc.

Library of Congress Cataloging-in-Publication Data

Bozzo, Linda.
    Getting around in the past, present, and future / Linda Bozzo.
      p. cm. — (Imagining the future)
    Includes index.
    Summary: "Readers will learn about the history, present, and dream about the possible
        futures of different types of transportation, including cars, planes, motorcycles, trains,
        bicycles, ships, trucks, and buses"—Provided by publisher.
    ISBN 978-0-7660-3437-2
    1. Motor vehicles—Juvenile literature. 2. Transportation—Juvenile literature. I. Title.
    TL147.B686 2011
    629.04—dc22
                            2010011596

Printed in the United States of America
052010 Lake Book Manufacturing, Inc., Melrose Park, IL

10 9 8 7 6 5 4 3 2 1

Illustration Credits: Courtesy of George Eastman House, pp. 12 (top), 22 (top); Everett
Collection, pp. 2, 6 (top), 18 (top), 20 (top);©iStockphoto.com/M_D_A, p. 10 (bottom); Tom
LaBaff, pp. 1, 7, 9, 11, 13, 15, 17, 19, 21; Library of Congress, pp. 4, 8 (top), 10 (top), 16 (top);
Shutterstock.com, pp. 3, 5, 6 (bottom), 8 (bottom), 12 (bottom), 14 (bottom), 16 (bottom), 18
(bottom), 20 (bottom), 22 (bottom); State Library and Archive of Florida, p. 14 (top).

Cover Illustrations: front cover—Tom LaBaff; back cover—Courtesy of George Eastman House
(bottom inset); Shutterstock.com (top inset).

CONTENTS

The History of Transportation 4

1 Cars 6

2 Airplanes 8

3 Motorcycles 10

4 Trains 12

5 Bicycles 14

6 Ships 16

7 Trucks 18

8 Buses 20

Words to Know 22

Learn More:
Books and Web Sites 23

Index 24

The History of Transporatation

Yesterday

Transportation is the way people and things are moved from place to place. At one time, getting around was not easy. Carriages pulled by horses were a popular way to travel. People did not often travel far from home.

Today, transportation is faster and safer.
People fly through the air in jet airplanes.

Tomorrow How do you think people
will get around in the
future?

1. Cars

Yesterday

Did You Know?

The first cars were known as "horseless carriages."

Thin wheels and dirt roads made for a bumpy ride in early cars. The driver's side was on the right.

Today, better tires and **paved** roads make for smoother rides. Now cars come in many sizes and colors. The driver's side is on the left.

Today

6

Tomorrow

What if some day cars did not need drivers? Just tell your car where you want to go. Want to visit a friend? How about some ice cream? The car will drive you there. What kind of car would you choose?

2. Airplanes

Yesterday

Long ago, airplanes could only carry one or two people.

Today

Today, airplanes are larger and more comfortable. They carry more people.

Tomorrow

One day, people might own small airplanes instead of cars. Running late for school? No need to worry. Jump in your airplane. BLAST! It takes off like a rocket from your roof. Enjoy your ride high above busy city streets. What might you see from up in the sky?

Yesterday

The first motorcycles looked like bicycles with **engines**.

Today

Today, motorcycles have lights and windshields. There are many different kinds to choose from.

Tomorrow

The motorcycle of the future might have a glass cover to guard the driver and **passengers** from rain. There would even be a special pet seat. What pet would you take for a ride on your motorcycle?

4. Trains

Yesterday

Early steam trains were very noisy.

Today

Today, electric trains are faster and quieter.

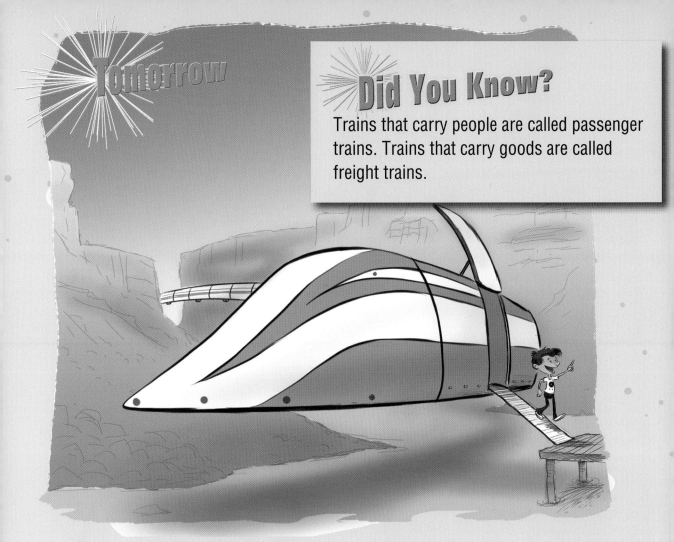

Did You Know?

Trains that carry people are called passenger trains. Trains that carry goods are called freight trains.

What if a train could pick you up at your front door? No train tracks? Do not worry. Trains may no longer travel on tracks. Trains may run on air instead. They will not make noise. The color of the train would tell you where it was going. Where would you go on a train?

5. Bicycles

Yesterday

Bicycles once looked like this. They made it easy for people who did not own cars to get around.

Today

Today, many people ride bicycles like this for exercise and fun.

Tomorrow

If you owned a bike many years from now, what might it look like? Maybe you could fold it up. You could store it in your backpack. What if you could make power pedaling your bike? How could you use that power in your home?

6. Ships

Yesterday

Ships are one of the oldest ways to move people and things.

Today

Many different types of ships are used today for transportation.

What if one day an entire city could be built on a ship? Would you like to live on the ocean? Ships might even use water as **fuel** to race across the waves. Would they ever run out of fuel?

7. Trucks

Yesterday

At one time, trucks were only able to move small, light loads.

Today

Today, trucks are much bigger. They can carry just about anything.

Tomorrow

Someday trucks may be big enough to carry your house. When you move, you would load your house on a truck. What if you could take your house anywhere in the world? Where would you want to go?

8. Buses

Yesterday

Many years ago, buses looked like large cars.

Today

Today's buses are bigger. They carry more people and use more fuel.

Someday the sun might power buses. This would save fuel and prevent **pollution**. Imagine a bus that bends going around corners. What if buses had a driver at both ends? Would buses ever have to turn around?

The world we live in is always changing. No one really knows what will happen in the future. We can only imagine!

WORDS TO KNOW

engines—Machines that make things move.

fuel—A material that is burned to make power.

future—The time after today.

passengers—People riding in a vehicle.

paved—A road that is covered with a hard material.

pollution—Materials harmful to air, water, and soil.

Books

Flatt, Lizann. *Let's Go: The Story of Getting From There to Here.* Toronto: Maple Tree Press, 2007.

Will, Sandra. *Transportation Inventions: From Subways to Submarines.* New York: Bearport Publishing, 2006.

Yates, Vicki. *Travel.* Chicago: Heinemann Library, 2008.

Web Sites

America on the Move
<http://americanhistory.si.edu/onthemove/games/>

PBS Kids GO! Wayback—Flight
<http://pbskids.org/wayback/flight/index.html>

INDEX

A

airplanes, 5, 8–9

B

bicycles, 10, 14–15
buses, 20–21

C

cars, 6, 7, 9, 14, 20
carriages, 4, 6

E

engine, 10

F

fuel, 17, 20, 21

M

motorcycles, 10–11

P

passenger, 11
pollution, 21

S

ships, 16–17

T

trains, 12–13
    freight trains, 13
    passenger trains,
    13
trucks, 18–19

W

Wright, Orville, 8
Wright, Wilbur, 8